A Note to Parents

DK READERS is a compelling program for beginning readers, designed in conjunction with leading literacy experts, including Dr. Linda Gambrell, Professor of Education at Clemson University. Dr. Gambrell has served as President of the National Reading Conference and the College Reading Association, and has recently been elected to serve as President of the International Reading Association.

Beautiful illustrations and superb full-color photographs combine with engaging, easy-to-read stories to offer a fresh approach to each subject in the series. Each DK READER is guaranteed to capture a child's interest while developing his or her reading skills, general knowledge, and love of reading.

The five levels of DK READERS are aimed at different reading abilities, enabling you to choose the books that are exactly right for your child:

Pre-level 1: Learning to read
Level 1: Beginning to read
Level 2: Beginning to read alone
Level 3: Reading alone
Level 4: Proficient readers

The "normal" age at which a child begins to read can be anywhere from three to eight years old, so these levels are only a general guideline.

No matter which level you select, you can be sure that you are helping your child learn to read, then read to learn!

LONDON, NEW YORK, MUNICH,
MELBOURNE, and DELHI

Series Editor Deborah Lock
Art Editor Clare Shedden
U.S. Editor John Searcy
Production Angela Graef
Picture Researcher Julia Harris-Voss
DTP Designer Almudena Díaz
Jacket Designer Emy Manby

Reading Consultant
Linda Gambrell, Ph.D.

First American Edition, 2006
06 07 08 09 10 10 9 8 7 6 5 4 3 2 1
Published in the United States by DK Publishing, Inc.
375 Hudson Street, New York, New York 10014

Published in Great Britain by Dorling Kindersley Limited

DK books are available at special discounts for bulk purchases
for sale promotions, premiums, fundraising, or educational use.
For details, contact:
DK Publishing Special Markets
375 Hudson Street
New York, New York 10014
SpecialSales@dk.com

Library of Congress Cataloging-in-Publication Data
Smith, Penny.
Animal hide and seek / written by Penny Smith.-- 1st American ed.
p. cm. -- (Dorling Kindersley level 1, beginning to read)
Includes index.
ISBN-13: 978-0-7566-1961-9 ISBN-10: 0-7566-1961-0 (pbk.) --
ISBN-13: 978-0-7566-1962-6 ISBN-10: 0-7566-1962-9 (hardcover)
1. Camouflage (Biology)--Juvenile literature. I. Title. II. Dorling
Kindersley readers. 1, Beginning to read.
QL759.S65 2006
591.47'2--dc22
2006006

Color reproduction by Colourscan, Singapore
Printed and bound in China by L Rex Printing Co., Ltd.

The publisher would like to thank the following for their kind
permission to reproduce their photographs:
Position key: a-above; b-below/bottom; c-center; l-left; r-right; t-top

Alamy Images: Agence Images 17; David Tipling 10tl; Aliki Sapountzi/
aliki image library 31br; Andre Seale 18-19; Blic Kwinkel 30br; Craig
Lovell/Eagle Visions Photography 26; Danita Delimont 15, 31tl; Michael
Patrick O'Neill 20-21; 18cl; FLPA 31tr; SCPhotos 11; Paul Souders 4;
Ardea.com: Piers Cavendish 29tr; Stefan Meyers 8t; **Corbis**: First Light
31bl; Kennan Ward 10bl, 32; Ralph A. Clavenger 30tl; Theo Allofs / Zefa
30bl; Tom Brakefield 7tr; **FLPA - images of nature**: Duncan Usher / Foto
Natura 8-9; Pete Oxford/Minden Pictures 14t; Shin Yoshino / Minden
Pictures 32t; Shin Yoshino/Minden Pictures 29cr; **naturepl.com**: 316 Simon
King 28-29; 12-13; **Science Photo Library**: Richard R Hansen 24
All other images © Dorling Kindersley
For further information see: www.dkimages.com

Discover more at
www.dk.com

Contents

BEGINNING
1
TO READ

Animal Hide and Seek

Written by Penny Smith

DK Publishing, Inc.

In the wild, some animals eat
other animals for food.
The animals hope their enemies
do not see them.
Some animals are covered
in patterns and colors.
They look like their surroundings.
This is called camouflage
[KAM-uh-flahj].

Comma
butterfly

Green
tree frog

Woodcock

5

In the shade of the woods,
a little fawn lies sleeping
next to a tree.
Its spotted coat makes it look
like a pile of fallen leaves.

fawn

8

Here is a family of wild boars.
A baby boar might make
a tasty meal for a wolf.
The babies have striped coats.
They are hard to see.

In the summer, the snowshoe hare
has red-brown fur.
In the winter, its fur grows thick
and white.
The hare crouches on the snow.
An owl flies overhead.
It does not see the still
and silent hare.

hare

This American dipper
waits near a mountain stream.
It is looking for insects to eat.
Its blue-gray feathers
make it hard to see
against the water.

insect

The gray fur of
the chinchillas [chin-CHILL-uhs]
keeps them hidden against
the rocks and stones.
Owls, foxes, and snakes
do not notice them there.

When this butterfly's wings are
closed, they are dark to blend in
with the shadows.
When it flutters, its wings
look like the eyes of a big animal.
This startles an enemy.
The butterfly has time
to fly away.

This pipefish beats its tiny fins
and swims among the branches
of underwater plants.
Can you see it?
It is not easy.

These decorator crabs
hook seaweed, stones,
and small sea creatures
onto their bodies.
The crabs are hidden.
As the crabs grow,
they crawl out of their shells.
They put the old decorations
onto their new shells.

In the rain forest, the chameleon
[kuh-MEEL-yun] is as green
as the branch it sits on.

It can change color to match
its surroundings.
It is hard for enemies to find.

Can you see the stick insect?
It is the same color and shape
as the dead leaves
on the forest floor.
The stick insect's eggs
look like seeds.

In the African grasslands, zebras graze together for safety. Their striped coats make it hard to tell one zebra from another.

Lions have trouble seeing
which one to attack.

lions

In the dry desert, a meerkat
sits up and sniffs the air.
Its silver-brown fur matches
the earth.

eagle

An eagle flies overhead.
The color of the meerkats' fur
makes it hard for the eagle
to see them.

Lots of animals are camouflaged.

They are hiding from you.

How many animals can you find?

Here are the answers:

1: looper moth, 2: gecko, 3: orchid mantis,
4: flounder, 5: ptarmigan [TAR-mi-gun],
6: tree frog, 7: leaf insect, 8: thorn bug, 9: seal.#7

Glossary

Eagle a large bird that hunts and eats smaller animals

Fawn a baby deer

Hare a large rabbit with long ears

Insect a small animal with six legs

Lions large, wild cats that live in Africa